Elias Hill
101 So Bad, They're Good Nurse Jokes
Copyright 2017
Self-published, Tiny Camel Books

Tiny Camel Books
tinycamelbooks.com
tinycamelbooks@gmail.com

101

So Bad, They're Good

Nurse Jokes

By: Elias Hill

Illustrations By: Katherine Hogan

Remember I'm a nurse,

the story needs to be extra good to gross me out.

I may need to
extend my lunch
break

into not working
here anymore.

Nurses are like icebergs,

at any time you only see 1/10 of what we are actually doing.

That awkward amount of time when you're trying to leave a patient's room,

but they won't stop talking.

When you hear a surgeon say he does amazing work,

yet you wouldn't trust him to cut butter.

The doctor doesn't need to examine your hand,

the pain is likely from you pressing the call button like you're tapping out Morse code.

When a family member tells me

their medical degree came from the University of Life Experience.

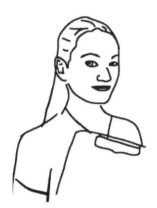

When you've had 3 admits, no lunch, need to pee and the charge nurse asks if you're OK.

I'm fine.

Your pain is 10/10?

Must be from pushing the IV pole down the sidewalk to go smoke.

Being a nurse is easy, it's like riding a bike.

Except the bike's on fire, and the ground is on fire. Everything is on fire because you're in hell.

Oh I'm sorry, mommy's a nurse.

We only go to the doctor when we're dying.

People who think laughter is the best medicine,

probably never had morphine.

Yay! It's the weekend!

Said no nurse ever.

And then I said,

"The doctor will be with you in a minute!"

My friends freak out over picking up dog poop.

Try changing a colostomy bag.

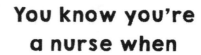

Elves and nurses have a lot in common.

We do all the work and a guy in an oversized coat gets all the credit.

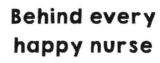

Behind every happy nurse

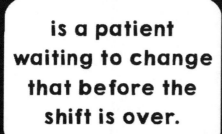

is a patient waiting to change that before the shift is over.

I don't often have naughty fantasies,

but when I do they usually involve soft music and waterboarding.

What will recovery be like?

Headaches, mood swings, anxiety, tiredness...

but don't worry, I'll get through it.

Anytime you see a picture of a nurse sitting down,

know that it's been Photoshopped.

I think I've diagnosed with the wrong illness.

According to the internet I have triachratochioris, a rare disease you get from a dinosaur.

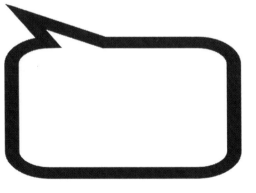

We have a Santa Clause who was admitted for fatigue. It seems he worked the entire holiday season with no time off!

Sounds familiar.

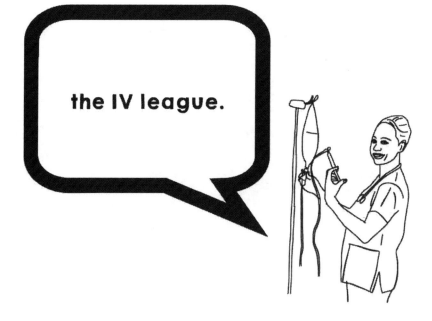

Ever since I gave that sponge bath to the chicken to prep it for dinner

my husband does all the cooking.

The doctor said he took an x-ray and it looked like it was broken.

And then I said, "Have you tried turning it off and on again?"

The doctor will be right with you.

What's taking so long?

He's getting his stethoscope out of the freezer.

How do you know when you've been a nurse too long?

You start to count the mistakes on medical shows.

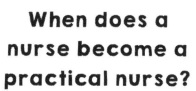

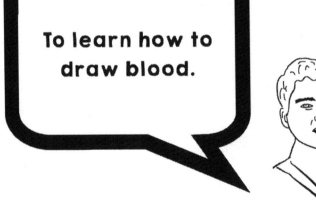

Hi. My name is Picaboo and I work in the Intensive Care Unit at a large hospital.

And when I answer the phone I get to say, "Picaboo, ICU."

How long does it take a doctor to change a lightbulb?

As long as it takes to find a nurse.

How long does it take for the nurse to change the light bulb?

30 seconds, but 45 minutes to document it.

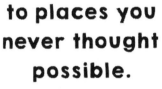

What I hope my patient looks like.

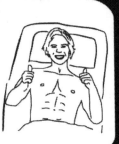

Why my patient actually looks like.

The fastest way to a switft punch in the throat

is to say, "It sure is quiet around here."

I tried to go a whole day without mentioning "bowels"

and failed.

The doctor may be cranky but his heart is in the right place.

We gave him an MRI just to be sure.

I am so excited the computer system is down and I get to use paper charts,

said no nurse ever.

No I don't lift weights,

I lift bodies.

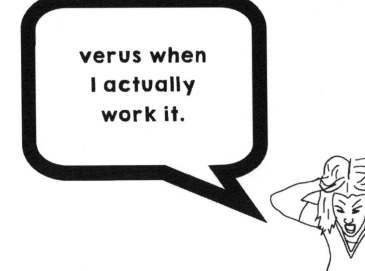

When my patient finally swallows

the last of his 27 morning meds.

I think I was stung by a wasp.

Whereabouts is it?

I'm sure miles away by now.

Adjusting your wife's pillows might make things more comfortable.

You're right,

I'll put them on my chair.

Keep pushing, honey, I can see the head!

Mr. Davis, that's your wife's head, you're at the wrong end.

Are we there yet? Are we there yet? Are we there yet?

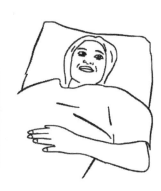

It's funny how my first born...

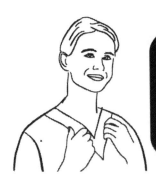

will actually be your second child.

Made in the USA
San Bernardino, CA
30 November 2018